I0440479

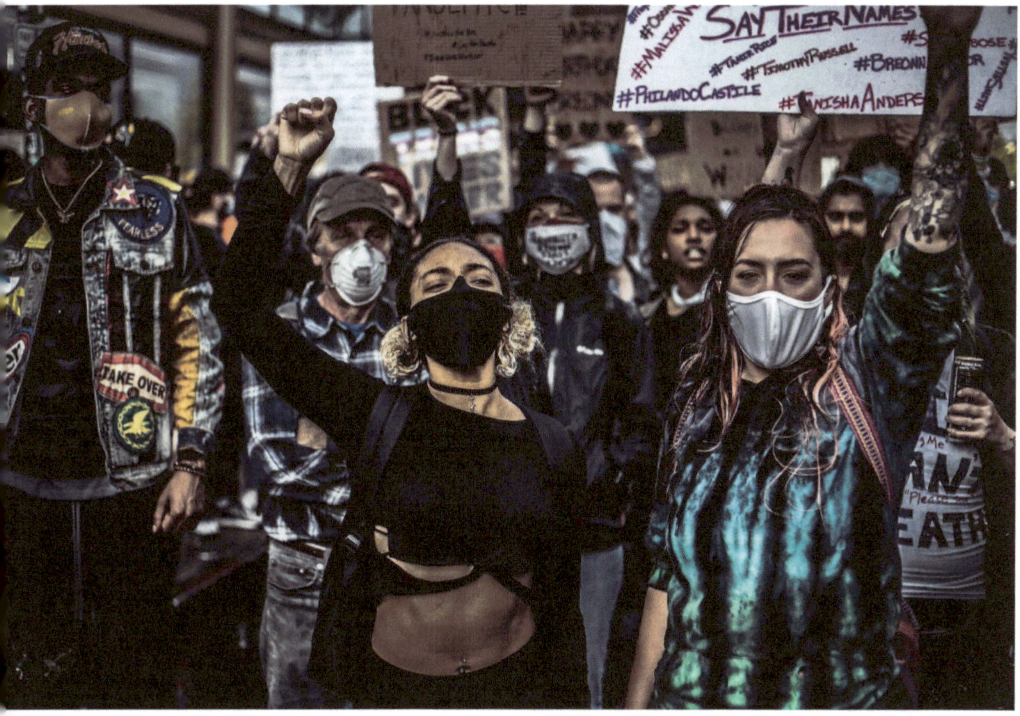
SAY THEIR NAMES
#PHILANDO CASTILE
#TIMOTHY RUSSELL
TAKE OVER
FEARLESS

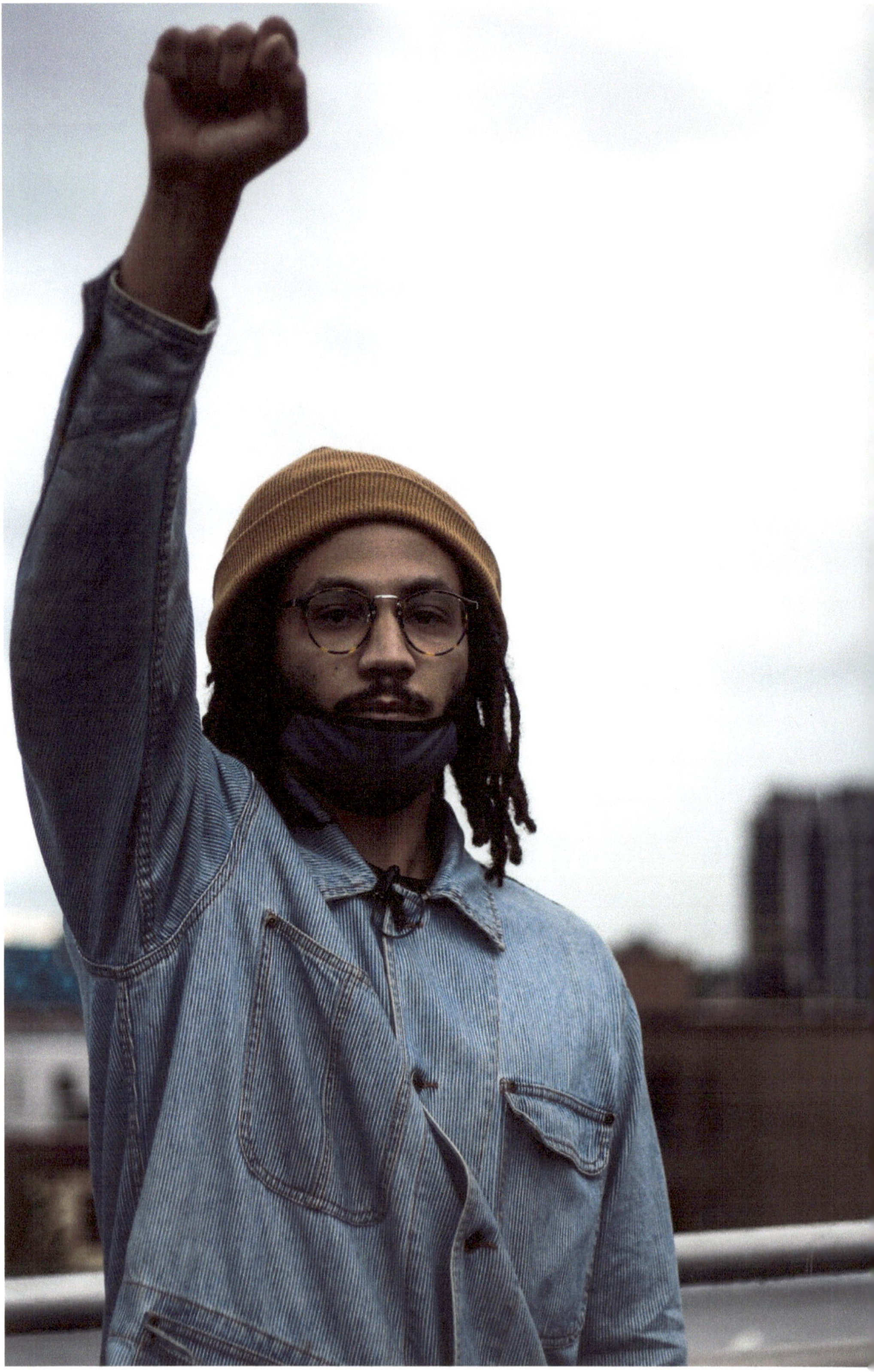

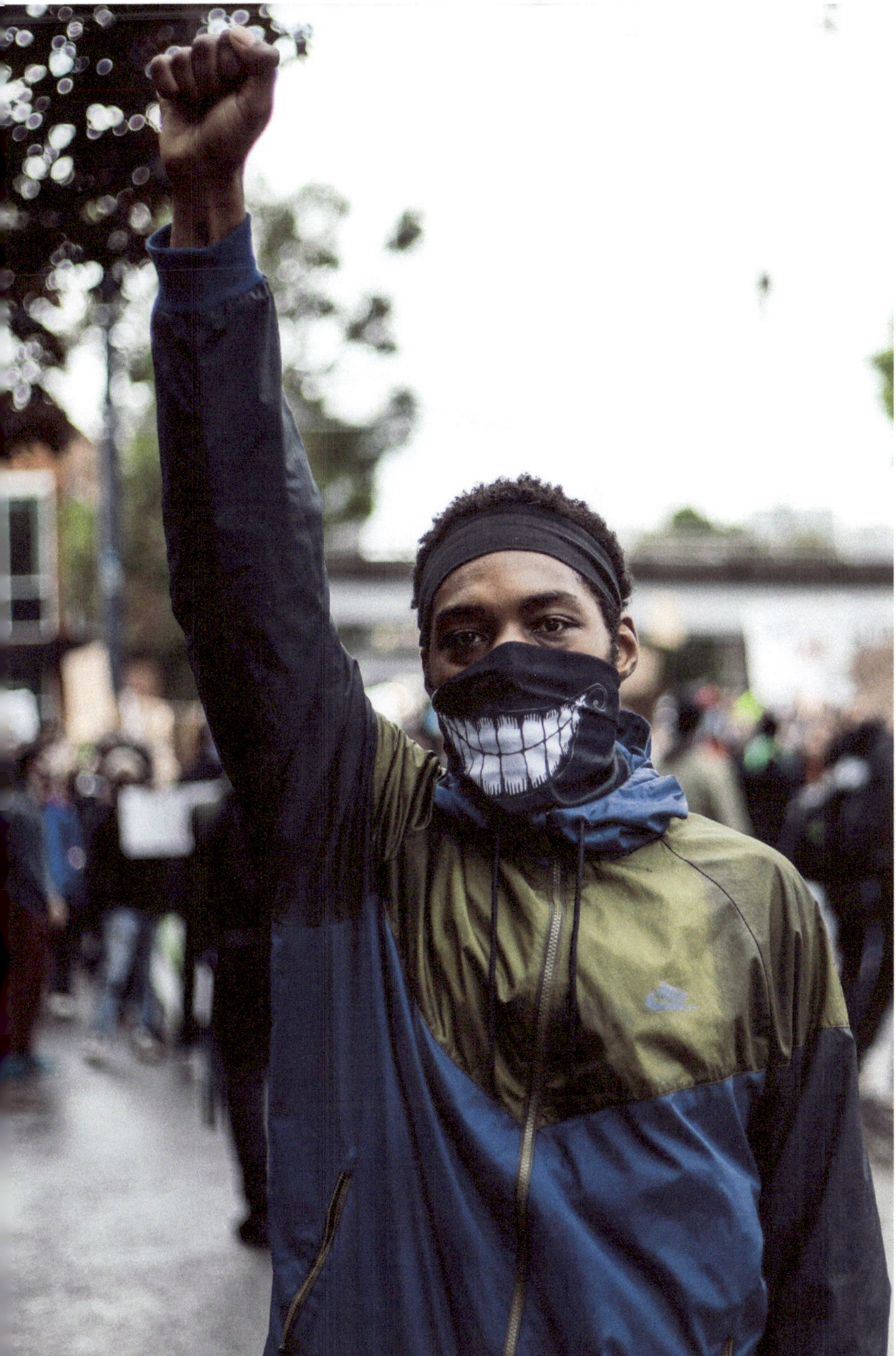

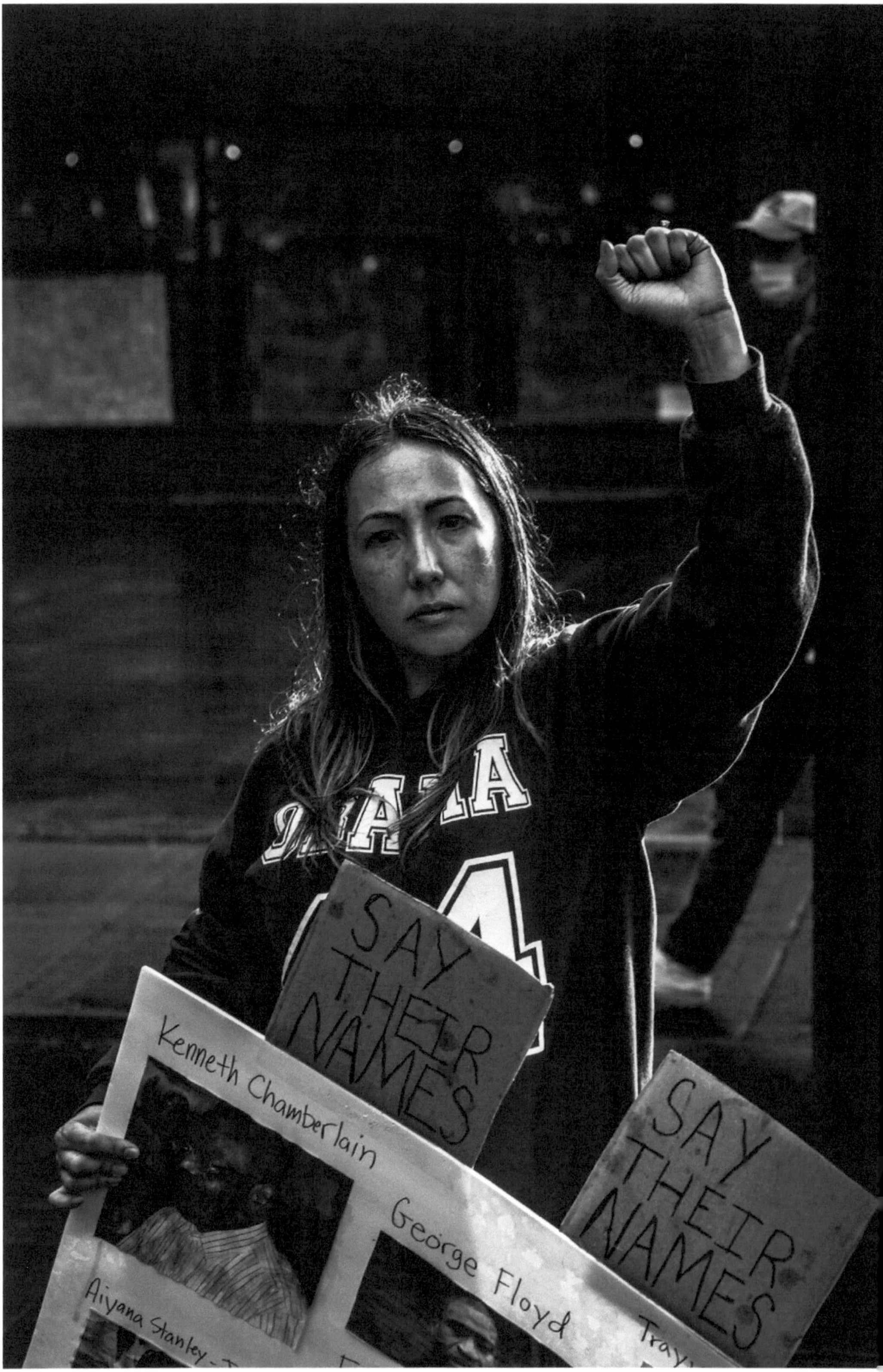
SAY THEIR NAMES
Kenneth Chamberlain
George Floyd
Aiyana Stanley
SAY THEIR NAMES

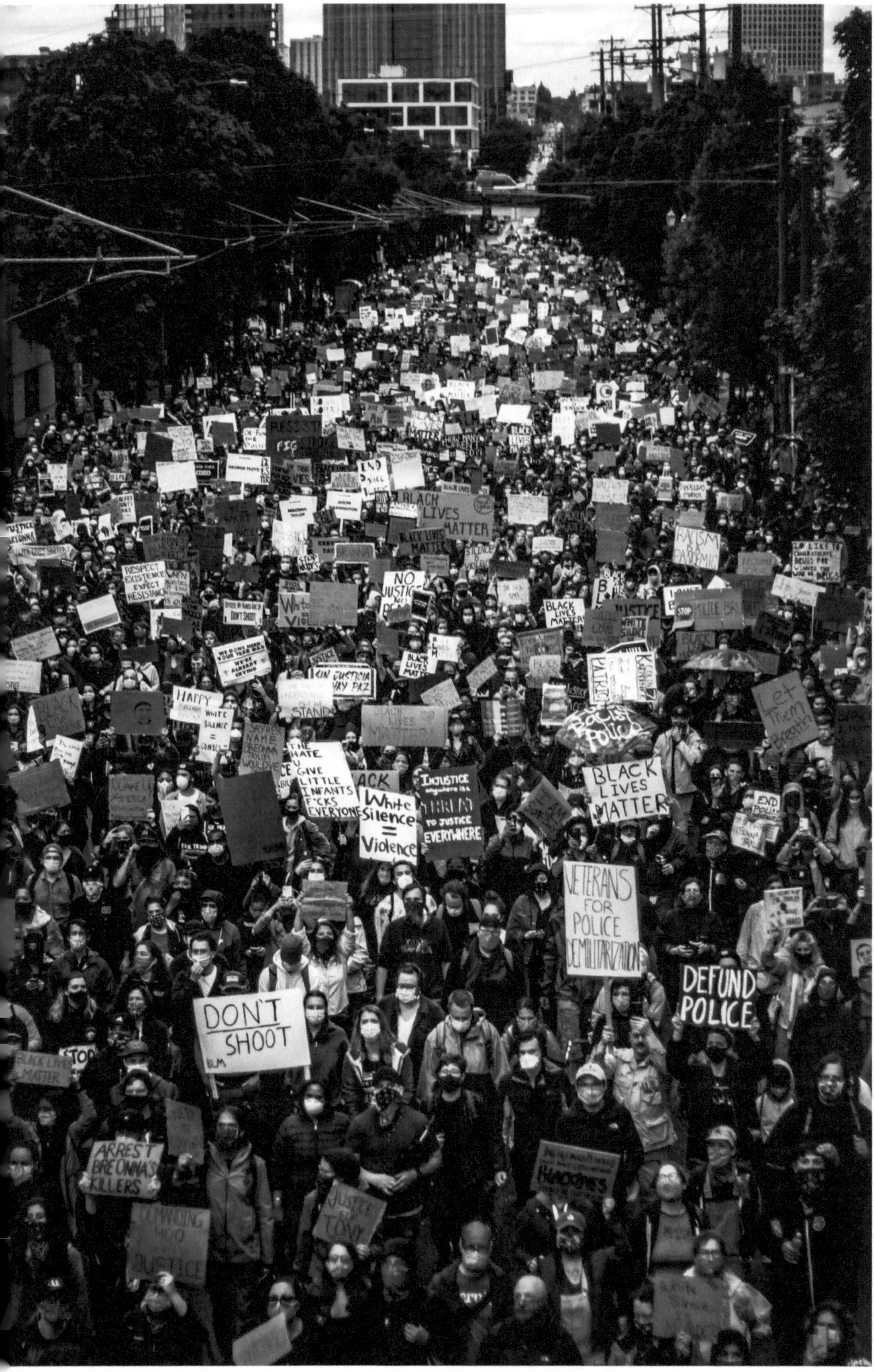
DON'T SHOOT
BLM
DEFUND POLICE
VETERANS FOR POLICE DEMILITARIZATION
BLACK LIVES MATTER
White Silence = Violence
INJUSTICE
TO JUSTICE EVERYWHERE
THE HATE U GIVE LITTLE INFANTS F*CKS EVERYONE
ARREST BREONNA'S KILLERS
RACISM IS A PANDEMIC
BLACK LIVES MATTER
Let Them Breathe
SIN JUSTICIA NO HAY PAZ
RESPECT EXISTENCE OR EXPECT RESISTANCE
BLACK LIVES MATTER
END POLICE

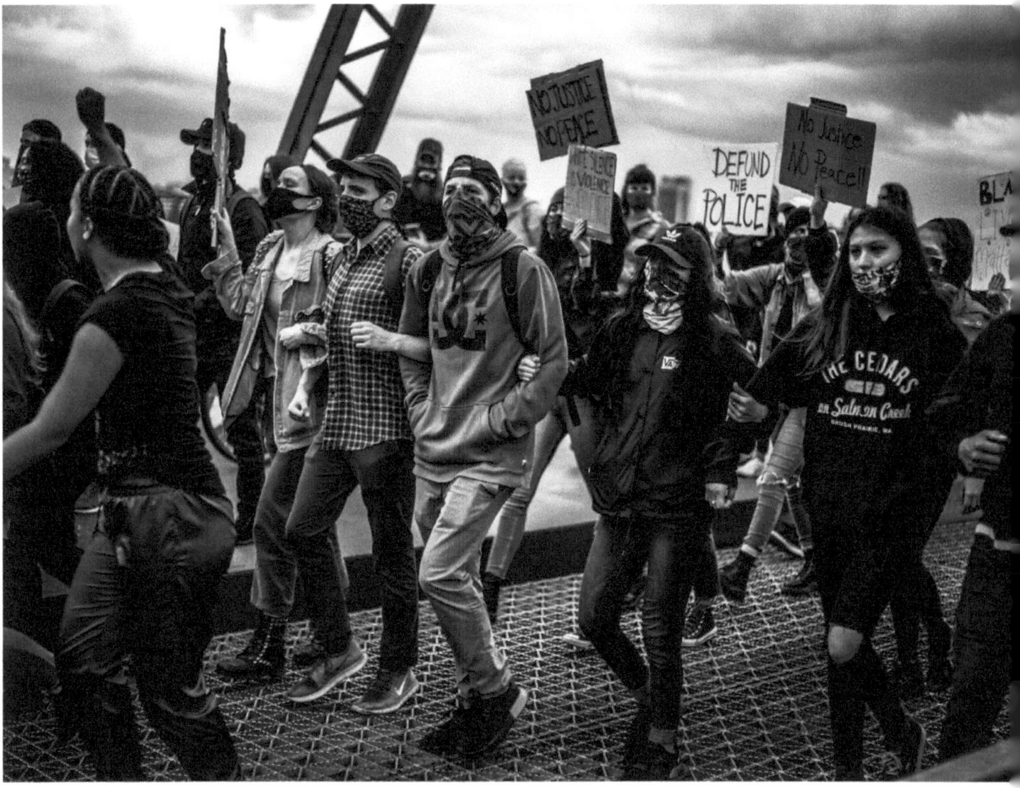
NO JUSTICE NO PEACE
DEFUND THE POLICE
No Justice No Peace!!
THE CEDARS

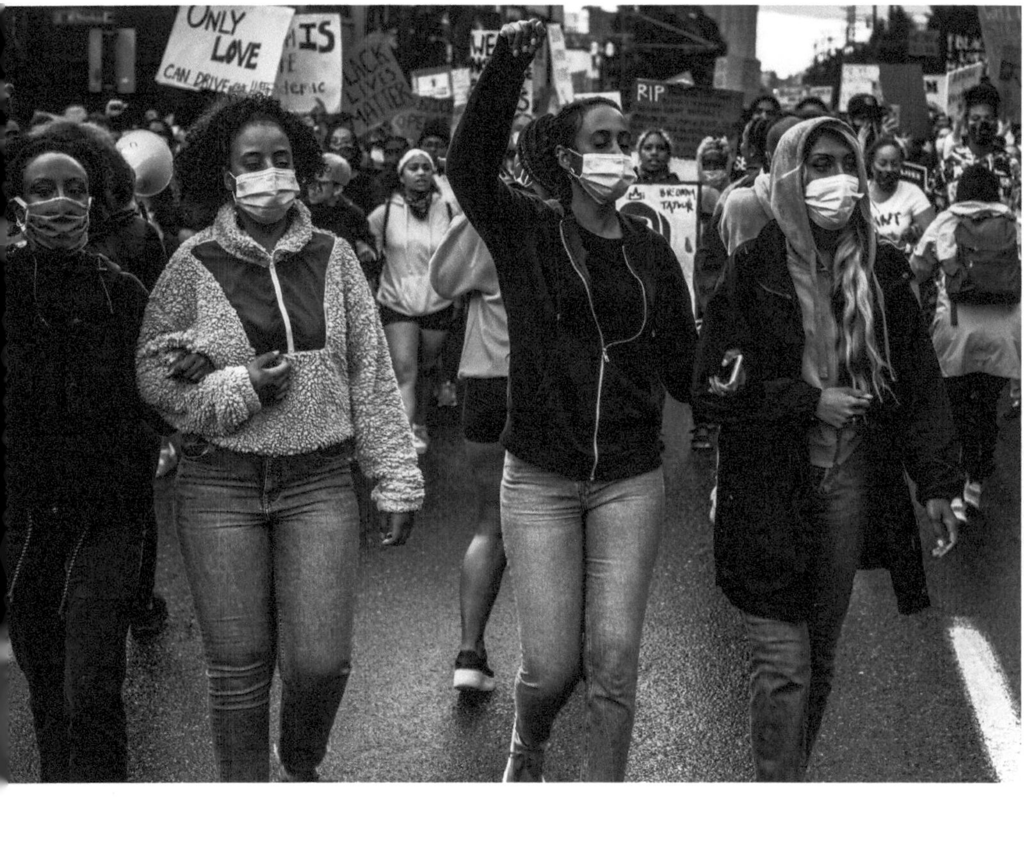
ONLY
LOVE
CAN DRIVE
RIP

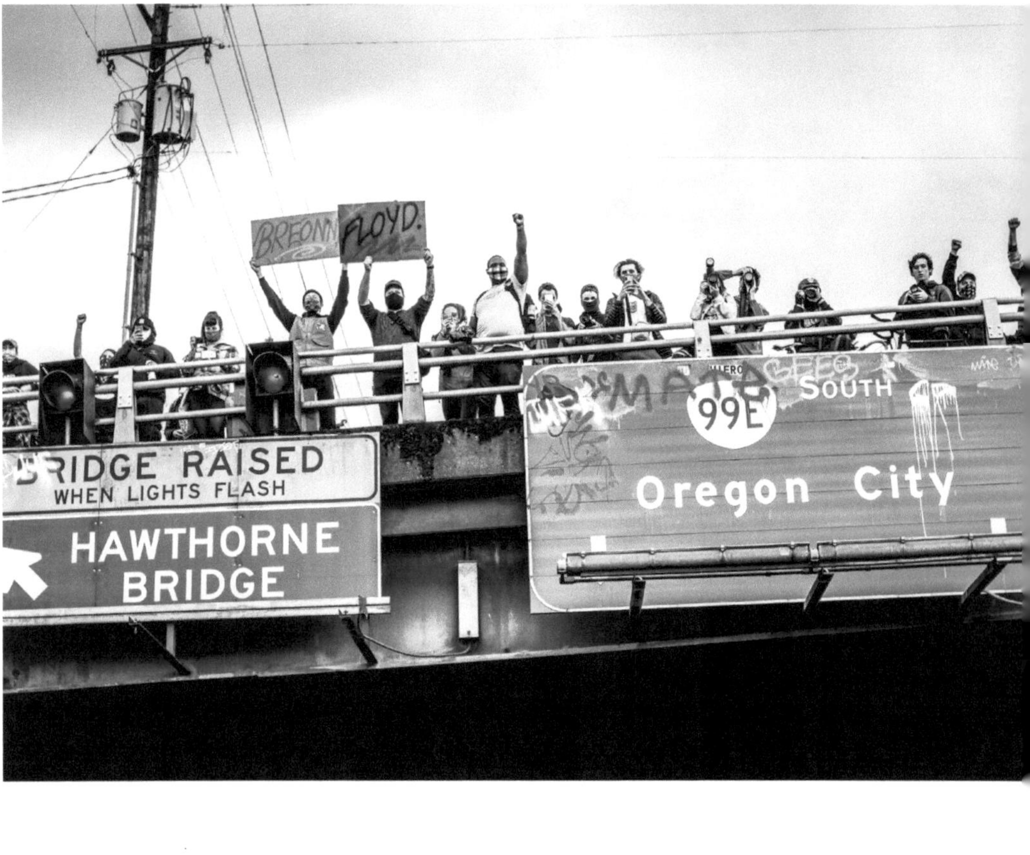
FLOYD.
BRIDGE RAISED
WHEN LIGHTS FLASH
HAWTHORNE
BRIDGE
99E
SOUTH
Oregon City

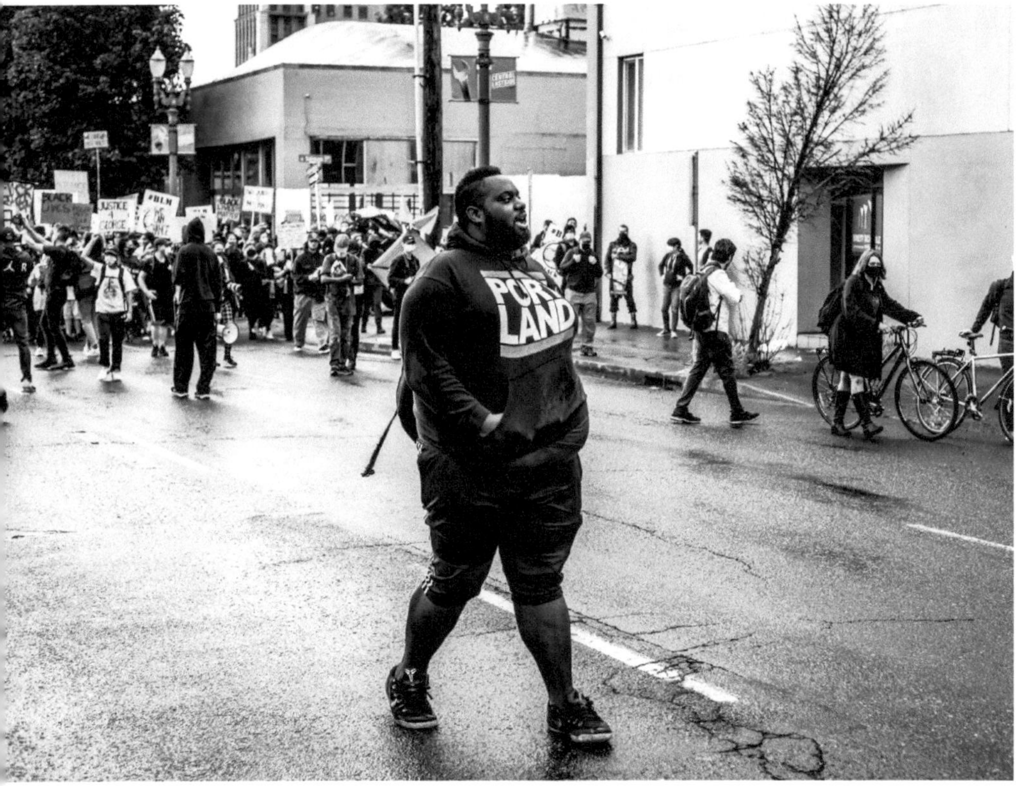
JUSTICE 4 GEORGE
#BLM
PORTLAND

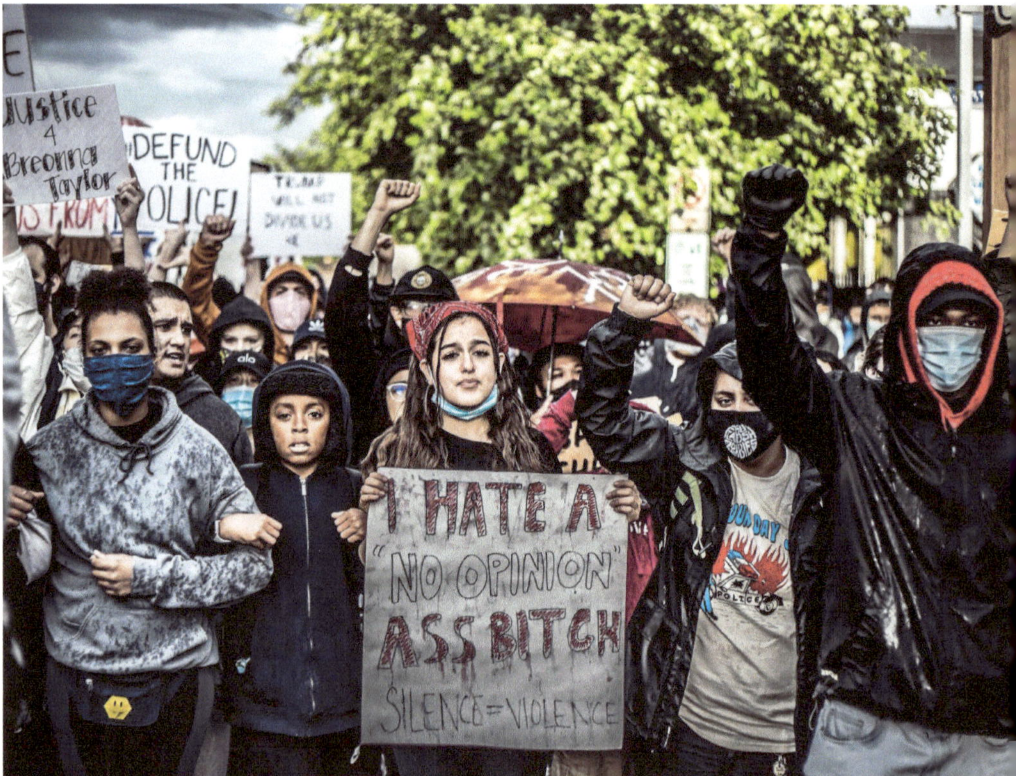
Justice 4 Breonna Taylor
DEFUND THE POLICE!
I HATE A "NO OPINION" ASS BITCH
SILENCE=VIOLENCE

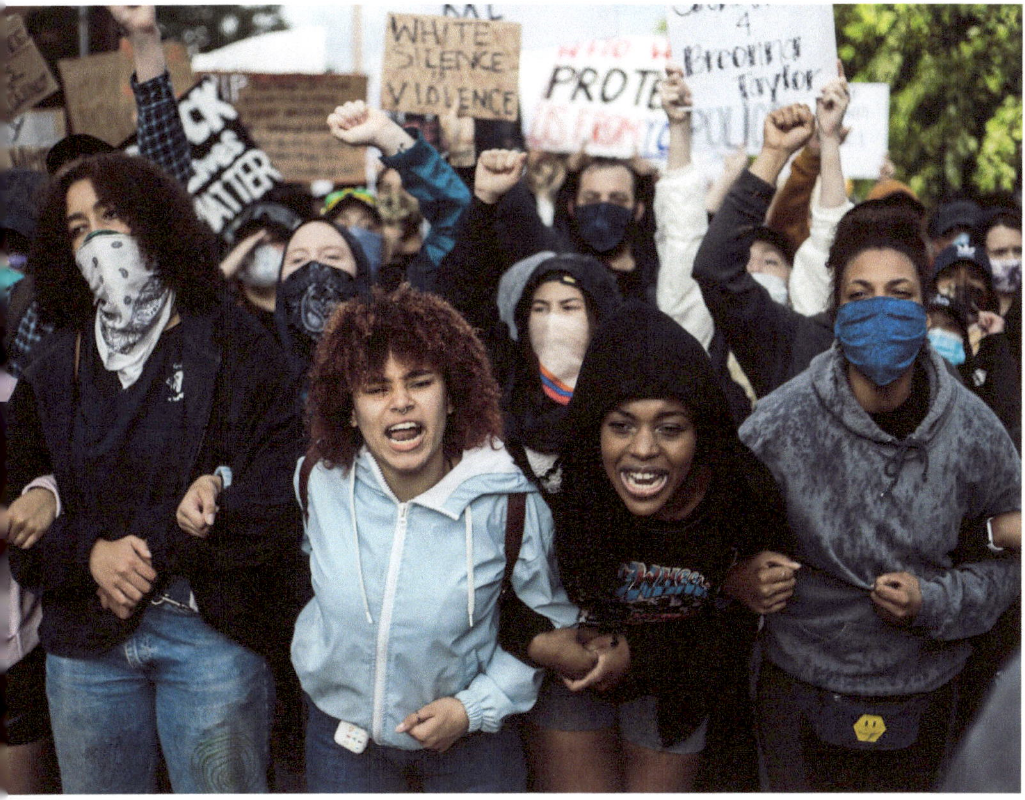
WHITE SILENCE IS VIOLENCE
4 Breonna Taylor

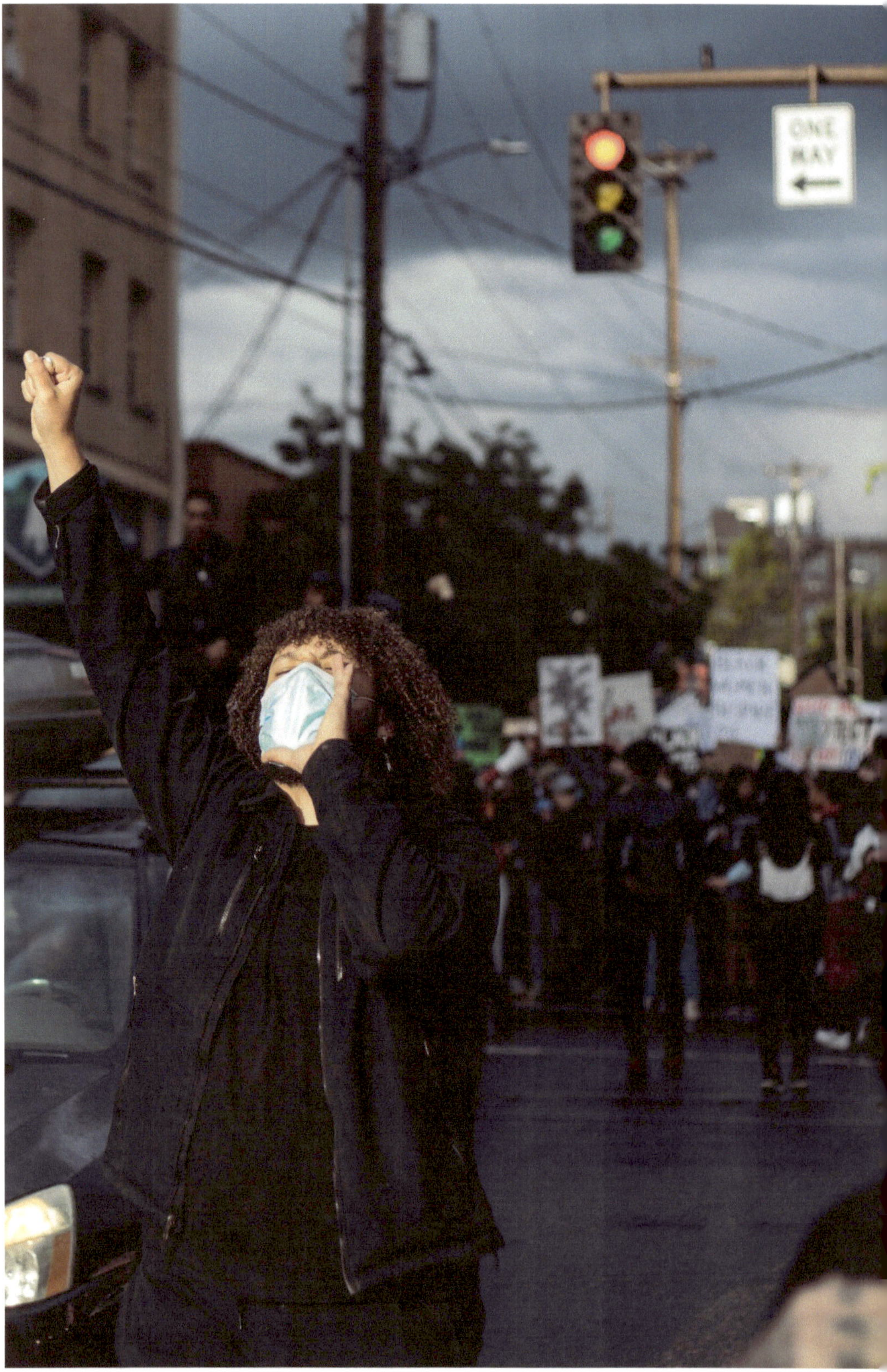
ONE
WAY

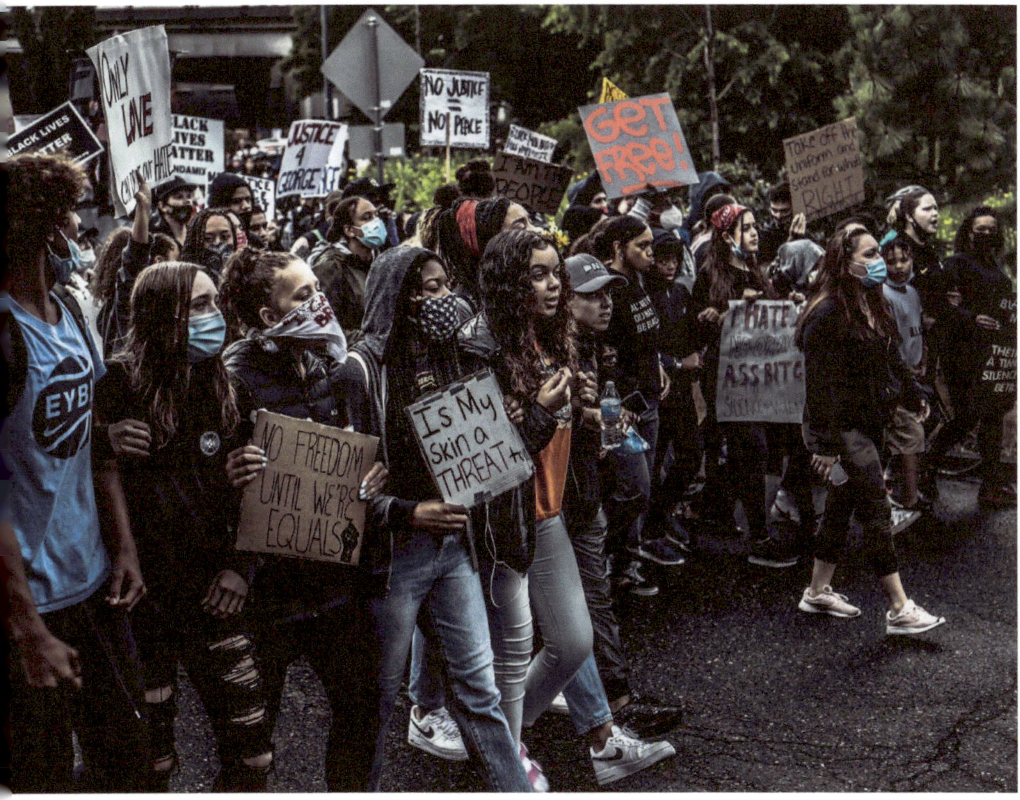
ONLY LOVE
BLACK LIVES MATTER
NO JUSTICE = NO PEACE
JUSTICE 4 GEORGE
GET FREE!
Take off the Uniform and Stand for what's RIGHT
NO FREEDOM UNTIL WE'RE EQUALS
Is My Skin a THREAT

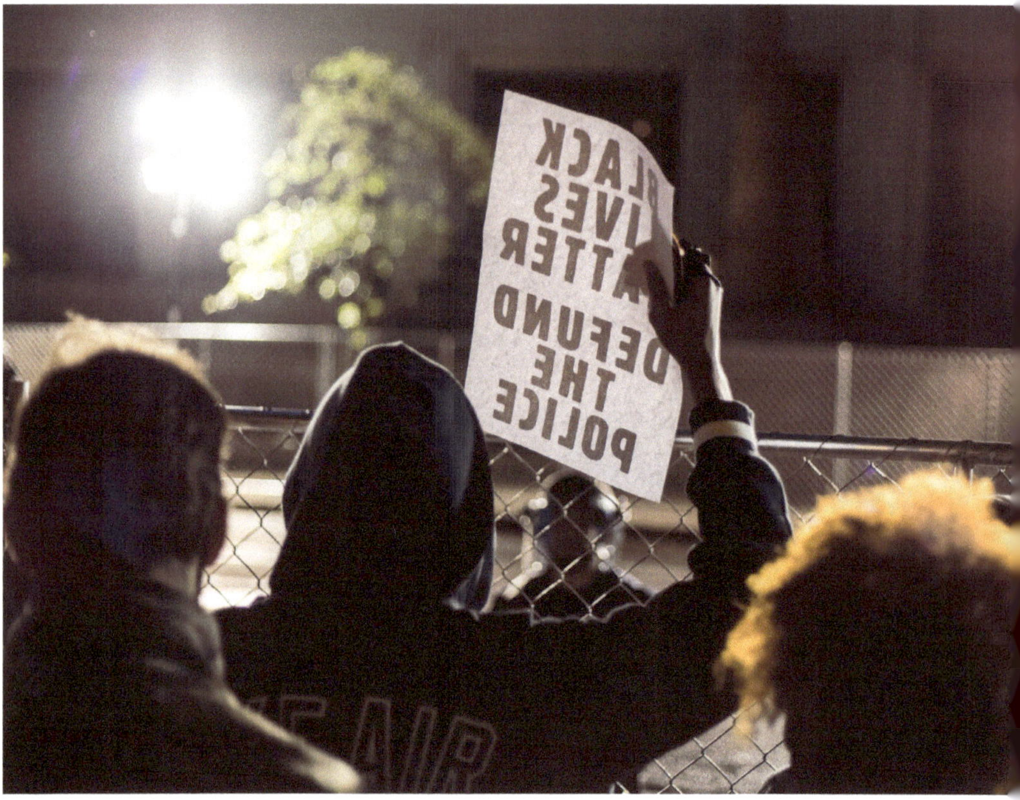
BLACK
IVES
ATTER
DEFUND
THE
POLICE

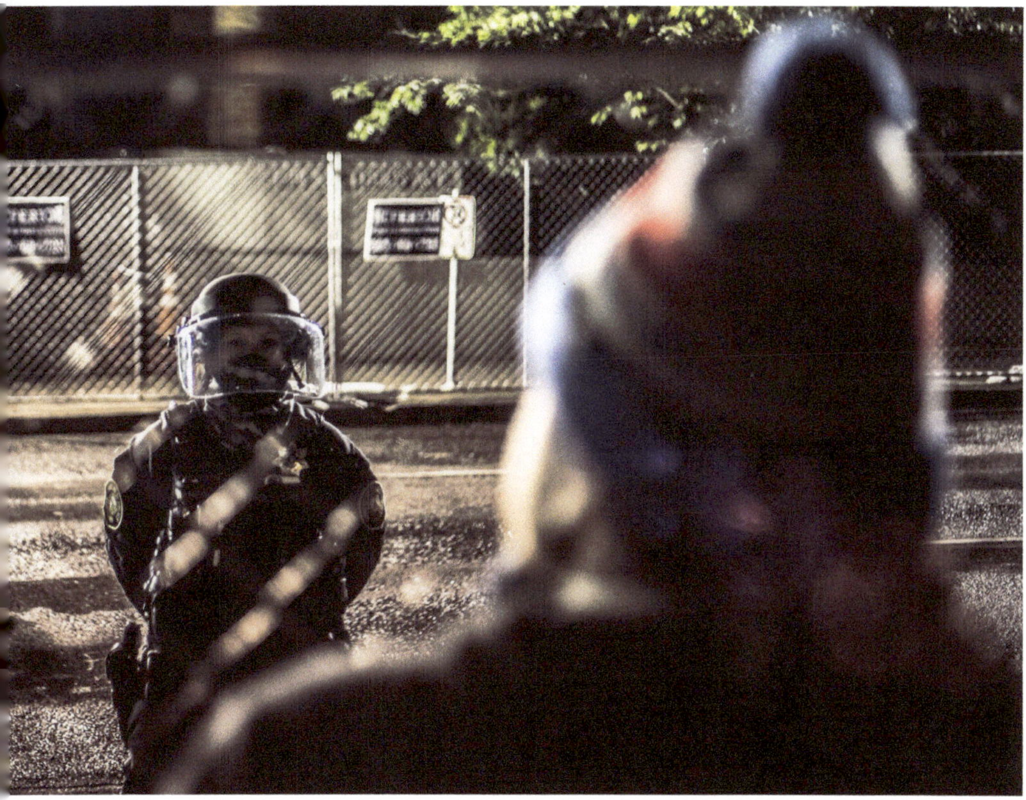

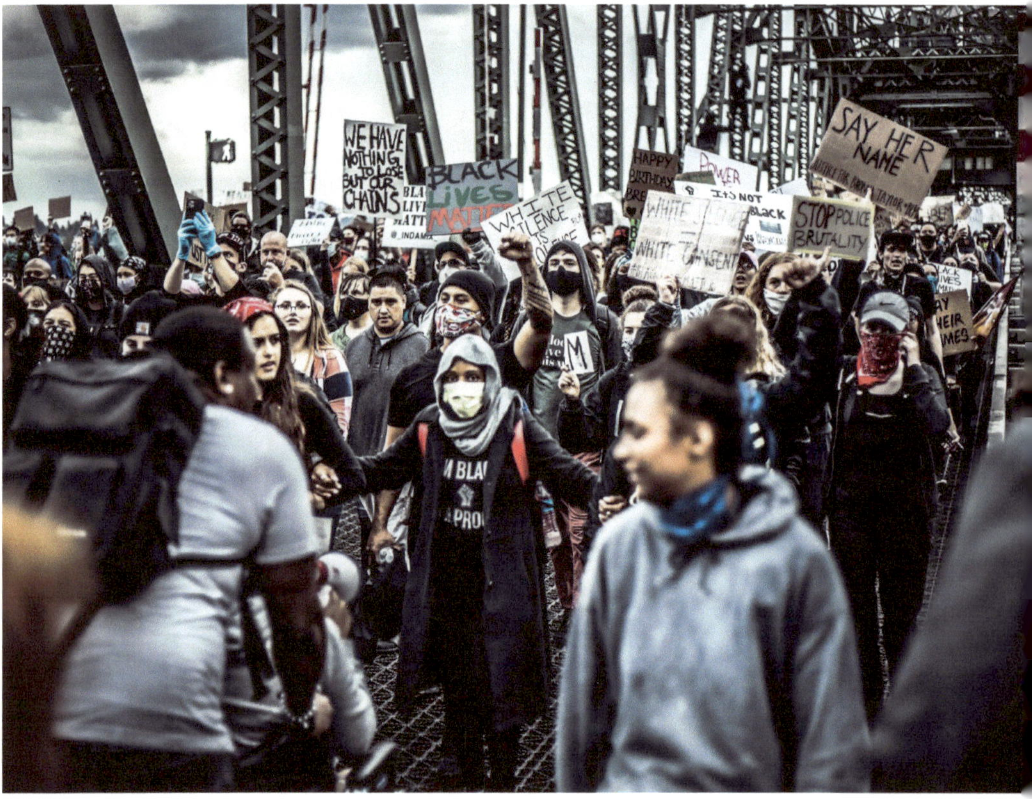
WE HAVE NOTHING TO LOSE BUT OUR CHAINS
BLACK LIVES
HAPPY BIRTHDAY
POWER
SAY HER NAME
STOP POLICE BRUTALITY

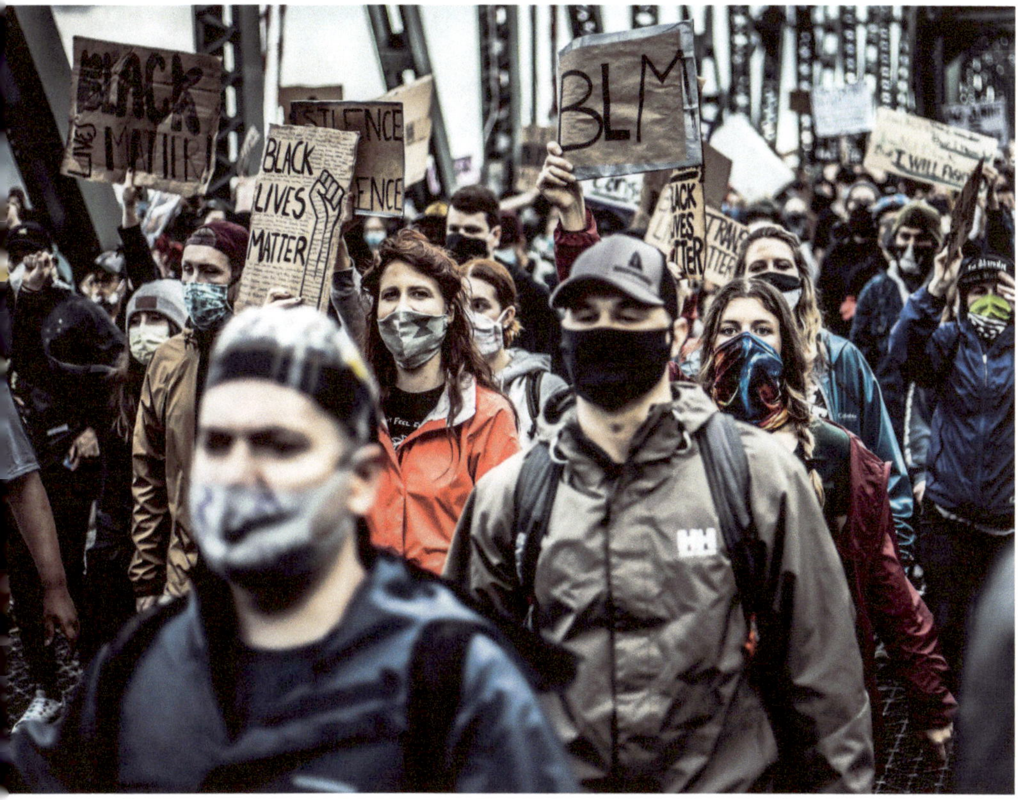
BLACK
LIVES
MATTER
BLM

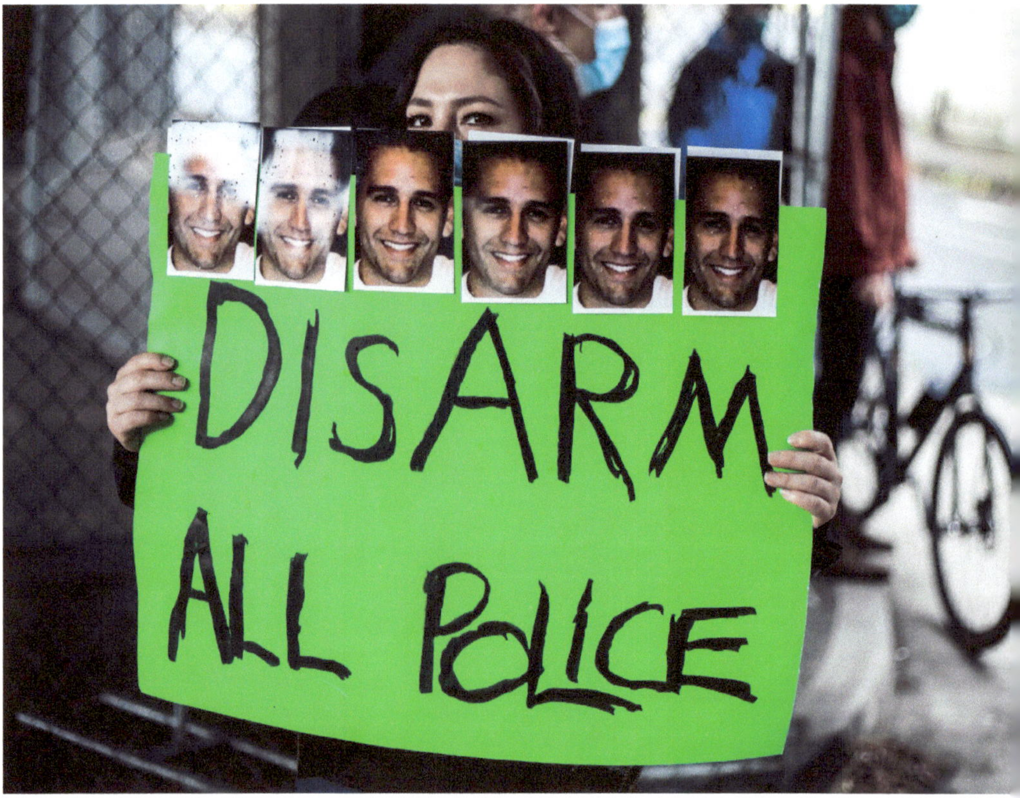
DISARM
ALL POLICE

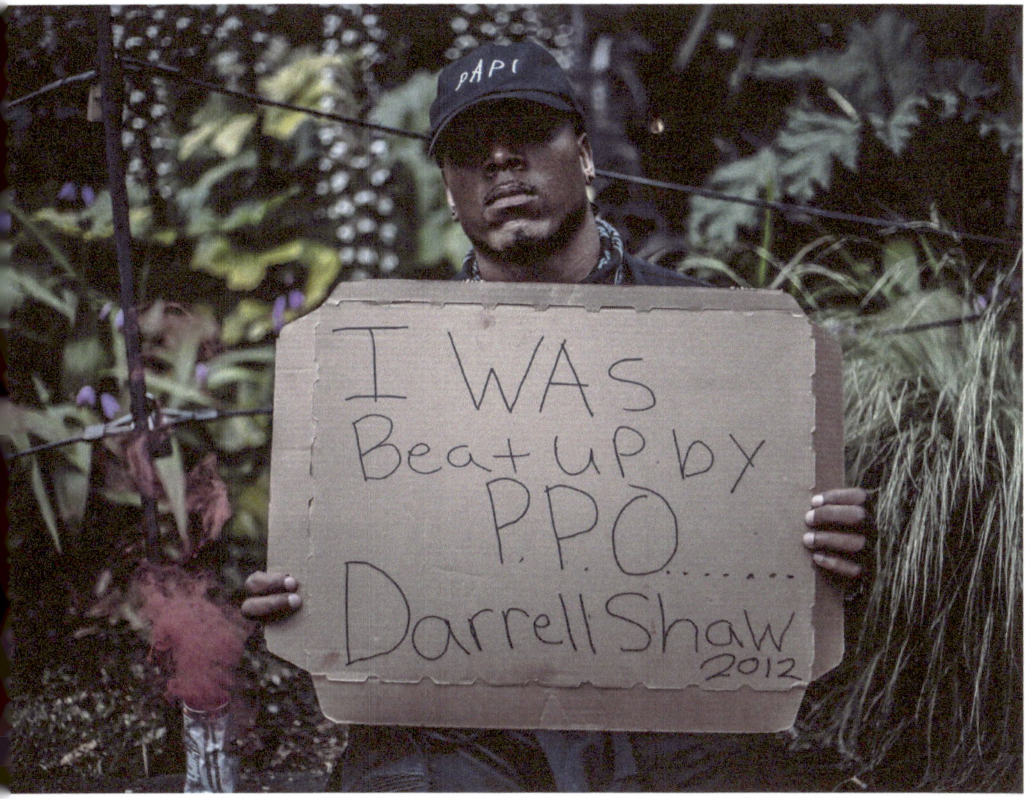
PAPI
I WAS
Beat up by
P.P.O
Darrell Shaw
2012

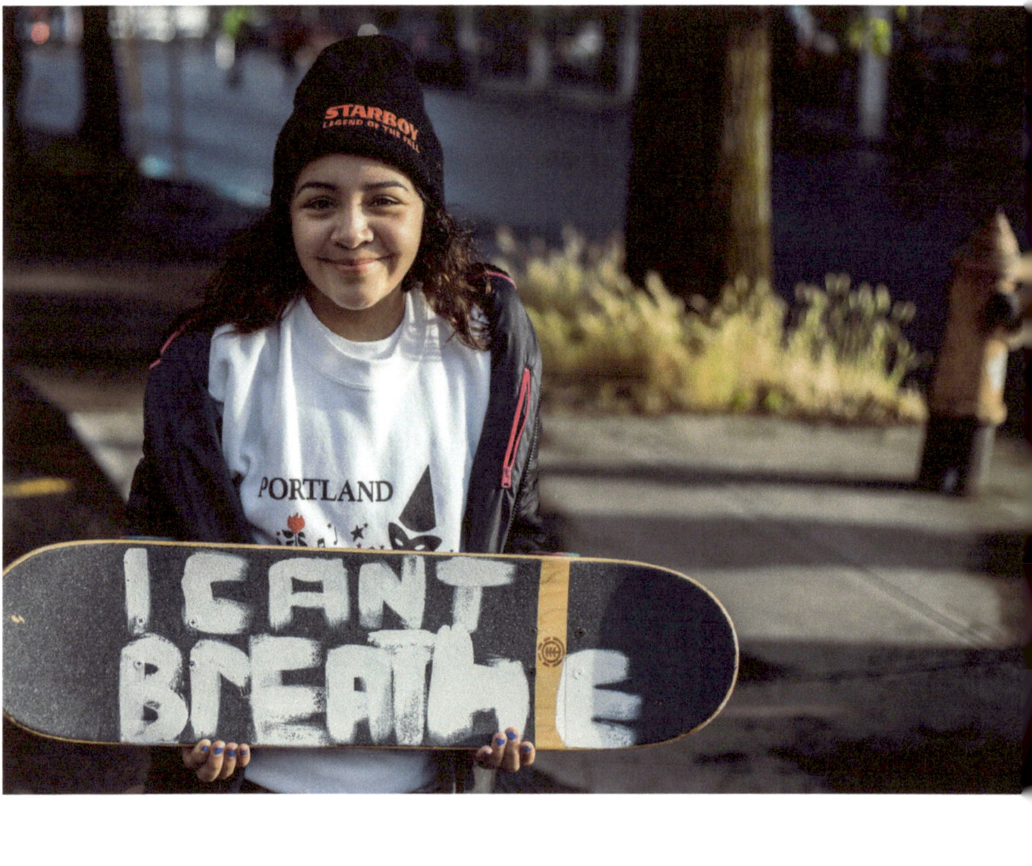
STARBOY
LEGEND OF THE FALL
PORTLAND
I CANT
BREATHE

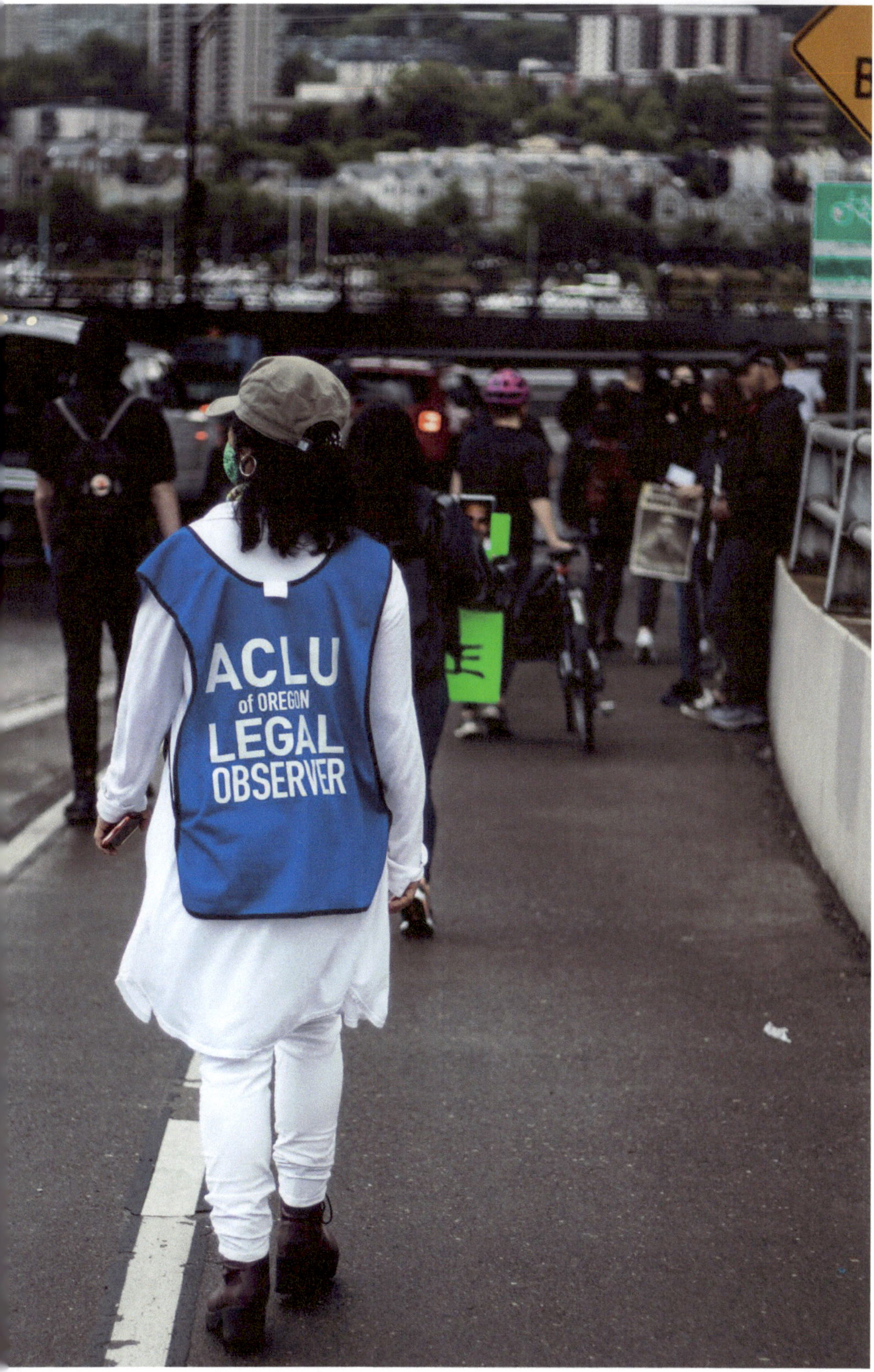
ACLU
of OREGON
LEGAL
OBSERVER

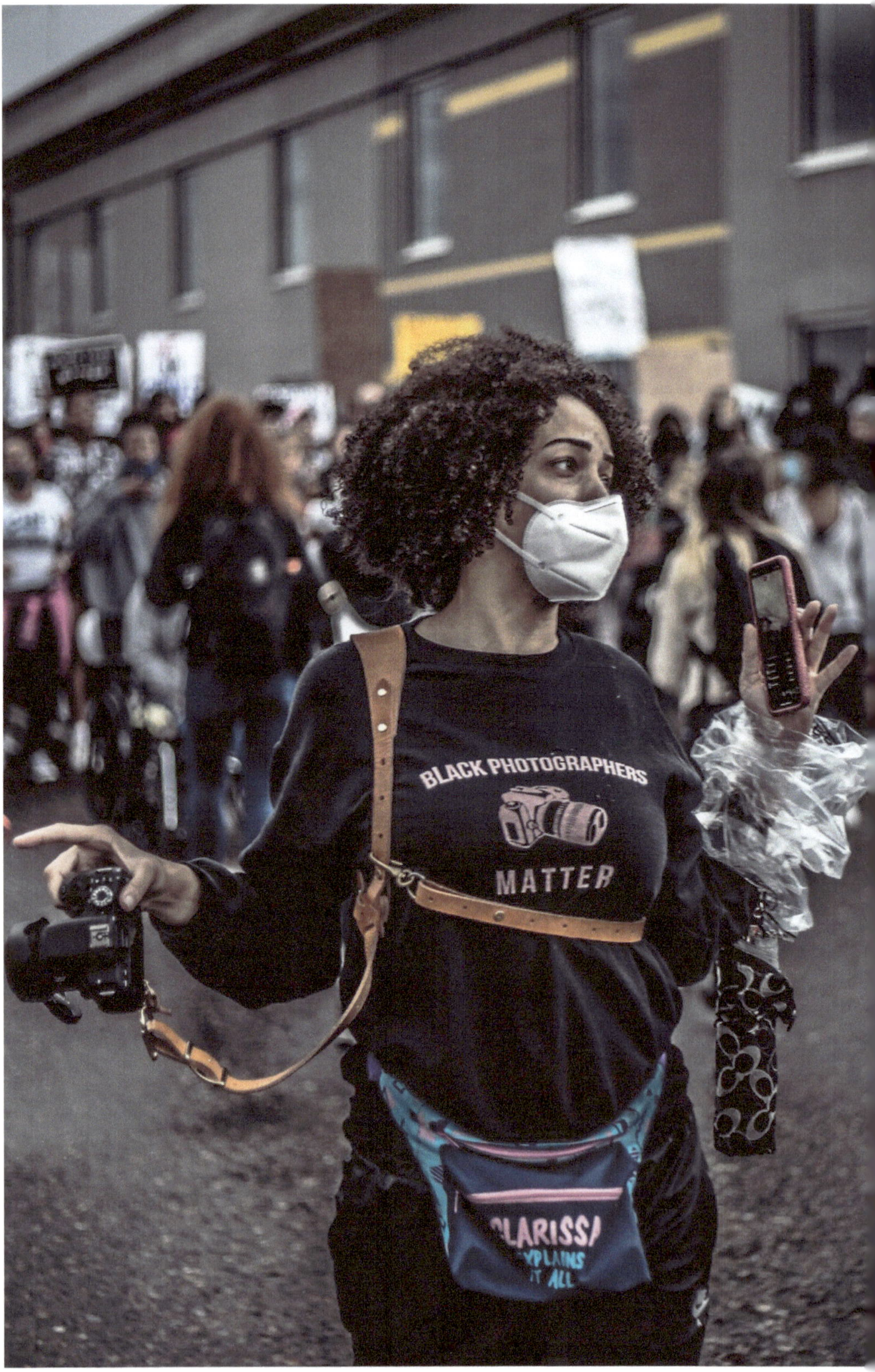
BLACK PHOTOGRAPHERS
MATTER

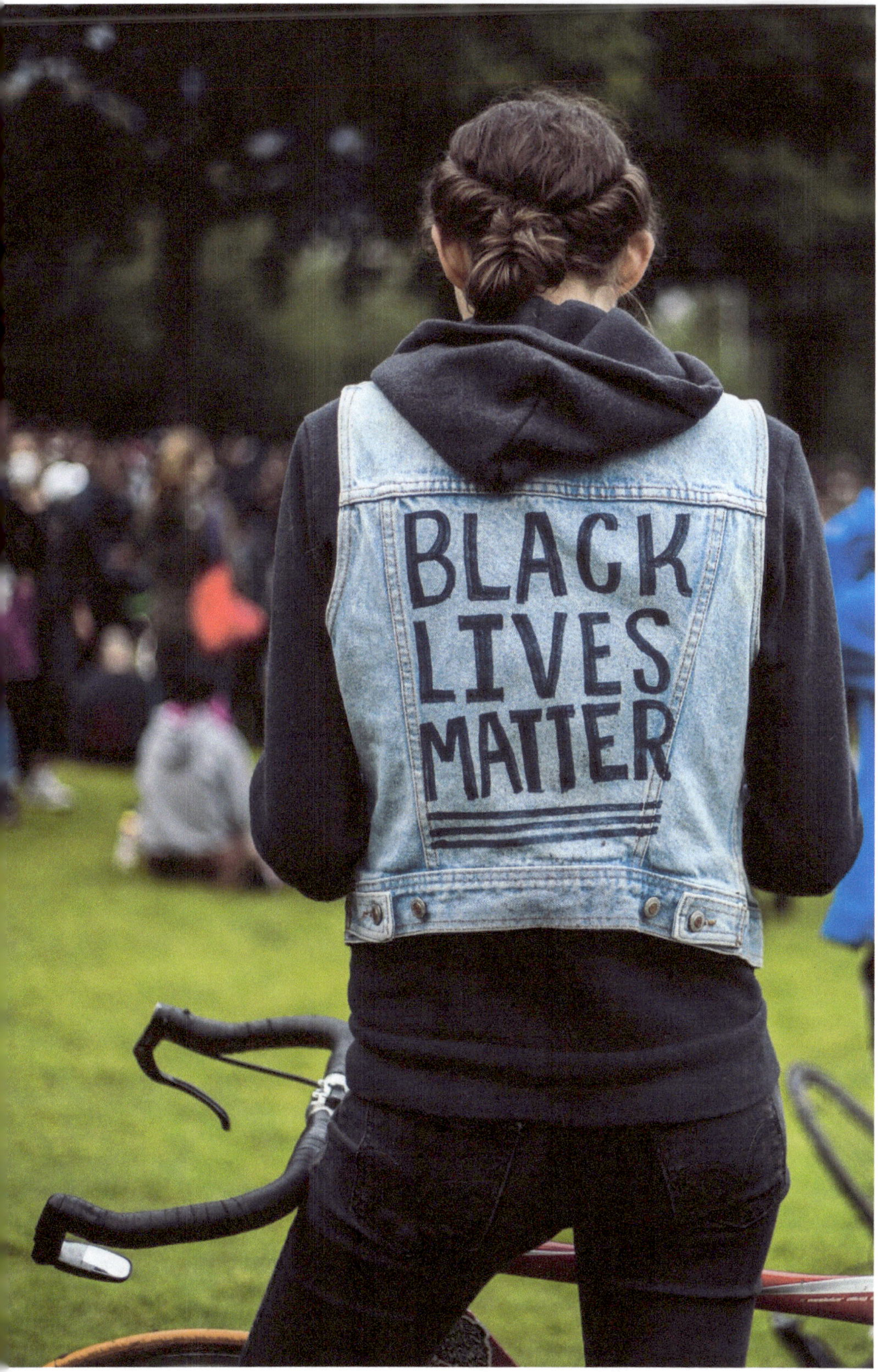
BLACK
LIVES
MATTER

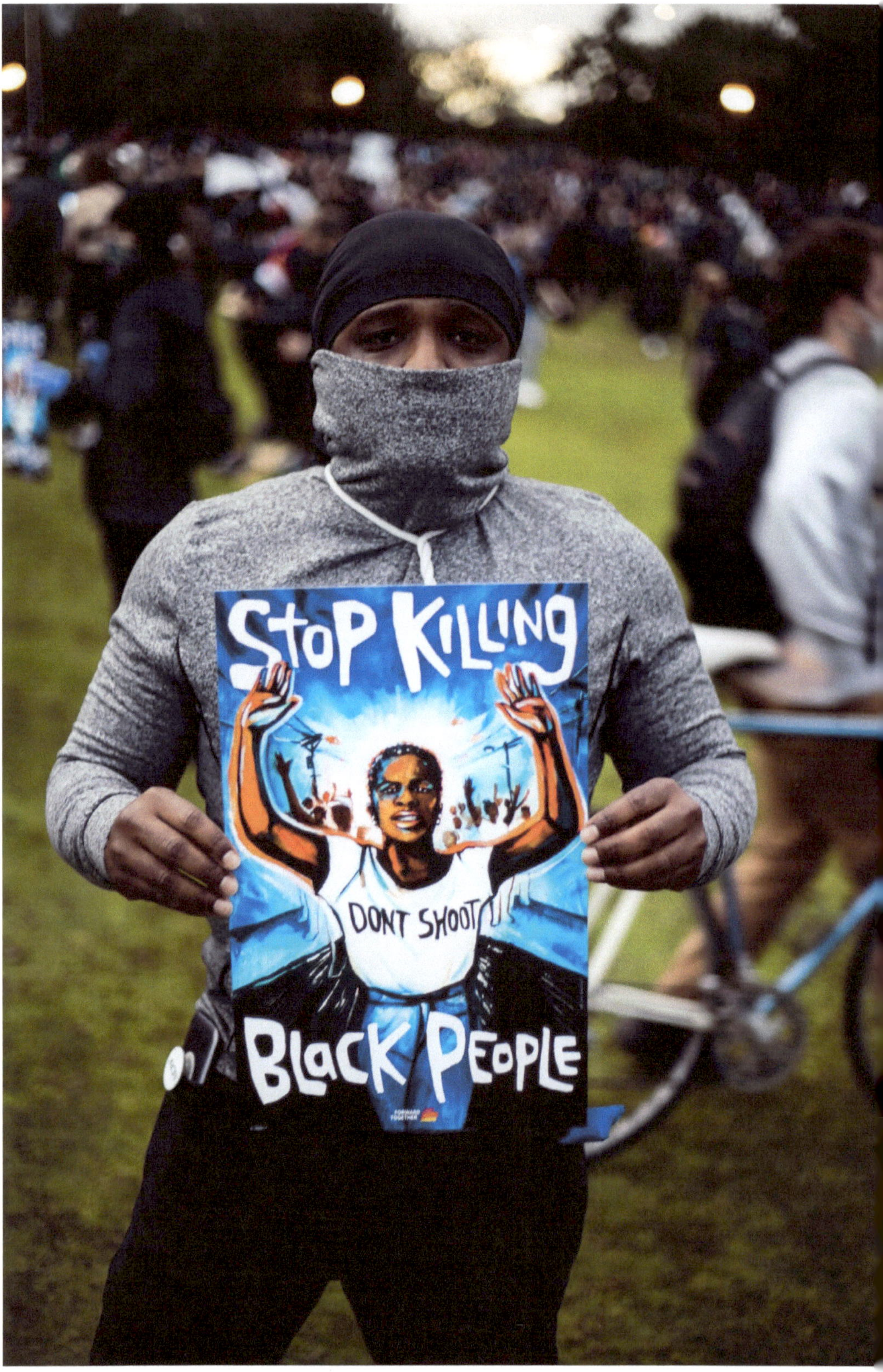
Stop Killing
DONT SHOOT
Black People

www.ingramcontent.com/pod-product-compliance
Lightning Source LLC
Chambersburg PA
CBHW040329010626
45792CB00024B/2318
*9798876432803*